ACHIEV LEVEL 5

MATHEMATICS

Fiona Mapp

RISING STARS

Rising Stars UK Ltd, 76 Farnaby Road, Bromley, BR1 4BH
www.risingstars-uk.com

Every effort has been made to trace copyright holders and obtain their permission for the use of copyright material. The authors and publishers will gladly receive information enabling them to rectify any error or omission in subsequent editions.

All facts are correct at time of going to press.

Published 2004
Text, design and layout © Rising Stars UK Ltd.

Editorial: Louise Moore/Chris Bellamy
Design: Button plc, London
Illustrations: Burville-Riley and Button plc
Cover photo: Getty Images
Cover design: Burville-Riley

British Library Cataloguing in Publication Data
A CIP record for this book is available from the British Library.

ISBN: 1-904591-31-0

Printed by Wyndeham Gait, Grimsby, UK.

Contents

HOW TO USE THIS BOOK

What we have included:

★ Those topics at Level 4 that are trickiest to get right.
★ All Level 5 content so you know that you are covering all the topics that you need to understand in order to achieve a Level 5.

 INTRODUCTION – This section tells you what you need to do to get to Level 5. It picks out the key learning objective and explains it simply to you.

 QUESTION – The question helps you to learn by doing. It is presented in a similar way to a SATs question and gives you a real example to work with.

 FLOW CHART – This shows you the steps to use when completing questions like this. Some of the advice appears on every flow chart (read the question then read it again). This is because this is the best way of getting good marks in the test.

 TIP BOXES – These provide test hints and general tips on the topic.

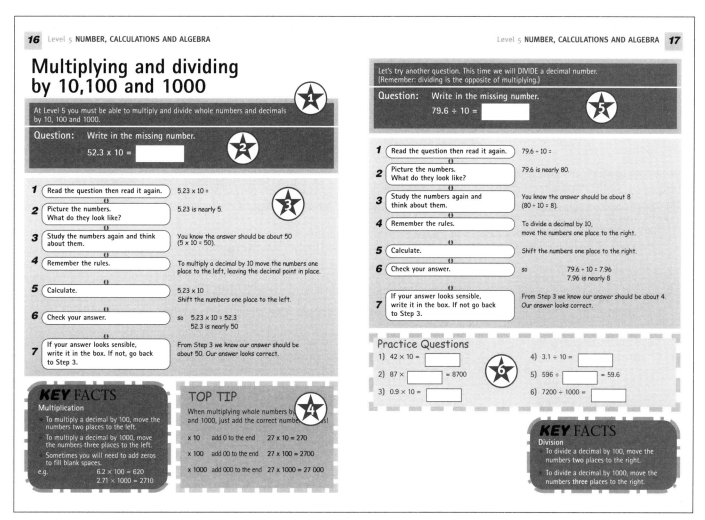

Multiplying and dividing by 10, 100 and 1000

At Level 5 you must be able to multiply and divide whole numbers and decimals by 10, 100 and 1000.

Question: Write in the missing number.

$52.3 \times 10 =$ ☐

1 Read the question then read it again. $5.23 \times 10 =$

2 Picture the numbers. What do they look like?   5.23 is nearly 5.

3 Study the numbers again and think about them.   You know the answer should be about 50 $(5 \times 10 = 50)$.

4 Remember the rules.   To multiply a decimal by 10 move the numbers one place to the left, leaving the decimal point in place.

5 Calculate. 5.23×10 Shift the numbers one place to the left.

6 Check your answer.   so $5.23 \times 10 = 52.3$ 52.3 is nearly 50

7 If your answer looks sensible, write it in the box. If not, go back to Step 3.   From Step 3 we know our answer should be about 50. Our answer looks correct.

KEY FACTS
Multiplication
* To multiply a decimal by 100, move the numbers two places to the left.
* To multiply a decimal by 1000, move the numbers three places to the left.
* Sometimes you will need to add zeros to fill blank spaces.
e.g. $6.2 \times 100 = 620$
$2.71 \times 1000 = 2710$

TOP TIP
When multiplying whole numbers by and 1000, just add the correct numbe s!
x 10   add 0 to the end $27 \times 10 = 270$
x 100   add 00 to the end $27 \times 100 = 2700$
x 1000   add 000 to the end $27 \times 1000 = 27\ 000$

Let's try another question. This time we will DIVIDE a decimal number. (Remember: dividing is the opposite of multiplying.)

Question: Write in the missing number.

$79.6 \div 10 =$ ☐

1 Read the question then read it again. $79.6 \div 10 =$

2 Picture the numbers. What do they look like?   79.6 is nearly 80.

3 Study the numbers again and think about them.   You know the answer should be about 8 $(80 \div 10 = 8)$.

4 Remember the rules.   To divide a decimal by 10, move the numbers one place to the right.

5 Calculate.   Shift the numbers one place to the right.

6 Check your answer.   so $79.6 \div 10 = 7.96$ 7.96 is nearly 8

7 If your answer looks sensible, write it in the box. If not go back to Step 3.   From Step 3 we know our answer should be about 4. Our answer looks correct.

Practice Questions

1) $42 \times 10 =$ ☐

2) $87 \times$ ☐ $= 8700$

3) $0.9 \times 10 =$ ☐

4) $3.1 \div 10 =$ ☐

5) $596 \div$ ☐ $= 59.6$

6) $7200 \div 1000 =$ ☐

KEY FACTS
Division
* To divide a decimal by 100, move the numbers two places to the right.
* To divide a decimal by 1000, move the numbers three places to the right.

SECOND QUESTION – On most pages there will be a second question. This will either look at a slightly different question type or give you another example to work through.

PRACTICE QUESTIONS – This is where you have to do the work! Try each question using the technique in the flow chart then check your answers at the back. Practising questions is the best way to help improve your understanding.

GOOD LUCK!

ACHIEVE LEVEL 5 MATHS – OBJECTIVES

This chart allows you to see which objectives in the National Numeracy Strategy have been covered. We have matched the objectives directly with each page of Achieve Level 5 so you can monitor progress. **Text in bold denotes key objectives.**

Page no.	Title	Objective
LEVEL 4 TRICKY BITS		
8	Predicting sequences	Recognise and extend number sequences formed by counting from any number in steps of constant size, extending beyond zero when counting back. (Numbers and the Number System)
9	Calculators	Enter numbers and interpret the display in different contexts. (Calculations)
10	Perimeter	Calculate the perimeter of shapes made of rectangles. (Measures)
11	The 24-hour clock	Use units of time; read the time on a 24 hour digital clock and use 24-hour clock notation, such as 17:05. (Measures)
12	Reading scales	Read and interpret scales on a range of measuring instruments. (Measures)
13	Multiples, factors and primes	Recognise and use multiples, factors (divisors), and primes. (Numbers and the Number System)
LEVEL 5 NUMBERS, CALCULATIONS AND ALGEBRA		
14–15	Checking your answers	Check results by inverse operations or rounding up and down.
16–17	Multiplying and dividing by 10, 100 and 1000	Understand and use decimal notation and place value, multiply and divide integers and decimals by 10, 100 and 1000.
18–9	Decimals	Add and subtract whole numbers and decimals to two decimal places. **Multiply and divide decimals with one or two places by single-digit whole numbers.**
20–21	Reducing fractions	Simplify fractions by cancelling all common factors and identify equivalent fractions.
22–23	Calculating fractions or percentages	Calculate simple percentages. Enter numbers and interpret the display in different contexts.
24–25	Multiplication and division	**Multiply and divide three-digit whole numbers by two-digit whole numbers.**
26–27	Negative numbers	Add and subtract positive and negative integers in context.
28–29	Simple formulae	**Use letter symbols to represent unknown numbers or variables. Understand that algebraic operations follow the same conventions and order as arithmetic operations.**
30–31	Understanding and simplifying expressions	Know the meaning of the word 'expression'. Simplify linear algebraic expressions by collecting like terms.

Page no.	Title	Objective
SHAPE, SPACE AND MEASURES		
32–34	Coordinates	Use conventions and notation for 2–D coordinates in all four quadrants; find coordinates of points determined by geometric information.
35–39	Angles	Use the correct vocabulary, notation and labelling conventions for lines, angles and shapes. **Know the sum of angles in a triangle.**
40–43	Reflection, rotation and translations	Understand and use the notation associated with reflections, rotations and translations.
44–45	Units of measure	Use units of measurement to estimate, calculate and solve problems in everyday contexts involving length, area, volume, capacity and mass. Know rough metric equivalents of imperial measures in daily use.
46–47	Estimating measures	Use units of measurement to estimate measures in everyday contexts involving length, area, volume, capacity and mass.
48–49	The area of a rectangle	Know and use the formula for the area of a rectangle, calculate the area of shapes made from rectangles.
HANDLING DATA		
50–53	Finding the mean, median, mode and range	Calculate statistics for small sets of discrete data; calculate the mean and find the mode, median and range.
54–55	Graphs and pie charts	Interpret diagrams and graphs (including pie charts) and draw simple conclusions.
56–57	The probability scale	**Understand and use the probability scale from 0 to 1.**

Predicting sequences

Predicting sequences is not as difficult as it sounds.

Just remember: sequence = numbers following a pattern.

Question: Predict the next two numbers in this sequence:

2, 10, 18, 26, __ , __

1 (Read the question then read it again.)   What is the pattern?

2 (Study the numbers.)   What is the difference between the numbers?
$2 + ? = 10$ $? = 8$
$10 + ? = 18$ $? = 8$

3 (Test the pattern.)   Is the difference between all the numbers 8?

2		10		18		26		34		42
	+8		+8		+8		+8		+8	

4 (Does the sequence work? If so, write in the next two numbers.)   Yes, the pattern works and the next numbers in the sequence are 34 and 42.

Pattern 1
The pattern may mean the difference between numbers is always the same:

2		4		6		8		10
	+2		+2		+2		+2	

Pattern 2
The pattern may mean the difference between numbers changes according to a rule:

5		11		23		41		65
	+6		+12		+18		+24	

Practice Questions
Find the missing numbers in these sequences.

1) 12, 22, 32, 42, __, __   2) 2, 8, 32, __, 512, __   3) 100, 50, 25, __, __

TOP TIP 1
You will see the pattern more easily if you write in the numbers underneath the sequence.

4		14		34		64
	+10		+20		+30	

TOP TIP 2
A sequence may be shown in pictures. Just turn the pictures into numbers to help you see the pattern.

★   ★★   ★★   ★★★★
                   ★★   ★★★

It can be written as:

1		2		4		7
	+1		+2		+3	

Calculators

Calculators can be seen as the answer to everything in Maths. If used correctly they are a useful tool but when used incorrectly they can become a nightmare!

There are a number of steps you can follow to succeed with calculators.

1 (Read the question then read it again.)   Does the question need a calculator?
Can you work out the question in your head?

2 (Press the keys carefully and methodically.)   Think clearly. Talk through the calculation in your mind.

3 (Check the calculator display.)   Always check to see if you have pressed the right buttons.

4 (Make sure you press the equals key (=) after each calculation.)   Do not forget to do this!

5 (Does your final answer look sensible? If not, go back to Step 1.)   If you feel the need to redo a calculation, don't hold back. A couple of seconds redoing a sum could save you a couple of marks!

Practice Questions

Use your calculator to solve these problems:

1) 729 + 468 = ☐   4) 79 × 6.7 = ☐

2) 114 − 6.9 = ☐   5) 638 × 4.25 = ☐

3) 279 ÷ 9 = ☐   6) 729 ÷ 0.24 = ☐

TOP TIP 1

Don't forget to press the decimal point key when keying in decimal numbers.

3.5 =

TOP TIP 2

As you press each button, check to see what appears on the display.

Perimeter

Let's look at how to calculate the perimeter of a shape.

A common mistake is to forget one side of a shape when measuring it!

Question: What is the perimeter of this shape?

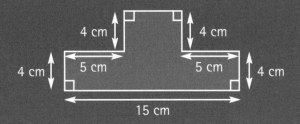

KEY FACTS
The perimeter is the total distance around the outside of a shape

1 Read the question then read it again.

What are we being asked to do? We are being asked to measure the distance around the shape.

2 Choose a side to start from. Put a line through it with your pencil.

This helps you to remember where you started from.

3 Add up all the lengths that are given in the question. Mark them off as you go.

4 + 5 + 4 + 4 + 5 + 4 + 15 = 41 cm

4 Now work out the lengths of the sides you haven't been given.

This is the IMPORTANT PART!
The right angles show you that the distance along the top of the shape must be the same as the distance along the bottom. Both must be 15 cm. The missing side must be 5 cm because 5 cm + 5 cm + 5 cm is 15 cm

5 Add the missing length to the total of the lengths you have been given (see Step 3).

41 cm + 5 cm = 46 cm

6 Is your answer a sensible one? If so, put it in the box.

The perimeter of the shape is 46 cm.

TOP TIP 1
Think of a perimeter fence going all the way round a football pitch.

TOP TIP 2
Don't try to measure 'missing' sides with a ruler. The reason they are missing is because the test wants to see if you can work it out from the given lengths.

The 24-hour clock

You should be pretty good at telling the time by now but certain questions can still cause problems. It is very easy to make silly mistakes when dealing with the 24-hour clock. When you are working out time it is important to take things step-by-step.

Question: How long is it from 02:13 to 21:15?

1 Read the question then read it again.

2 Picture the question.

Imagine the times –
02:13 is very early in the morning; 21:15 is late at night. The answer is going to be quite high.

3 Count the minutes round to the first hour.

02:13 to 03:00 is 47 minutes.

4 Now count the hours round to the given hour.

3:00 to 21:00 is 18 hours.

5 Add up the minutes and convert to hours if you need to.

47 minutes + the 15 minutes from the time 21:15 = 62 minutes.
62 minutes = 1 hour and 2 minutes.

6 Calculate all the hours and add the remaining minutes to give a final answer.

18 hours + 1 hour + 2 minutes = 19 hours and 2 minutes.

7 Does the answer look sensible? If so, put it in the box.

Yes. 19 hours and 2 minutes is correct.

Practice Questions

Work out the following times in hours and minutes:

1) 09:15 to 15:35

2) 07:14 to 19:20

3) 19:36 to 02:20

4) 22:07 to 23:28

TOP TIP 1 Get used to reading timetables for buses, trains and aeroplanes. Test yourself on imaginary journeys.

TOP TIP 2
Remember, when comparing times the **fastest** one is the **shortest** one.

Reading scales

We use scales to measure things. The tricky bit is remembering that you need to work out what each mark on the scale stands for.

Question: How much water is there in the measuring cylinder?

[   ] ml

1 Read the question then read it again.

2 Picture the numbers.

The answer is between 200 ml and 250 ml.

3 Study the scale.

Count the gaps made by the small lines between 200 ml and 250 ml.
There are 5 gaps. We therefore know that 5 gaps must equal 50 ml.

4 Calculate the scale.

5 gaps = 50 ml
1 gap = 10 ml (50 ÷ 5)

5 Answer the question.

Water level is at 200 ml plus 1 gap
       = 200 ml + 10 ml
       = 210 ml

6 If your answer looks sensible, write it in the box.

If not, go back to Step 2 and try again.

Practice Questions   How much water is in these measuring cylinders?

1)   [   ]

2)   [   ]

TOP TIP 1 Read scales very carefully and count the gaps more than once to be sure you have got it right. Write in missing measurements in pencil to help you remember them.

TOP TIP 2

Always check your answer carefully to be sure it makes sense.

Multiples, factors and primes

You should be able to use multiples, factors and primes.

Question: From this list of numbers, write down the multiples of
4, 12, 15, 4, 48, 33, 13

KEY FACTS 1

The **multiples** of 6 are 6, 12, 18, 24... This is just the 6 times table. A multiple is any number in the times table.

KEY FACTS 2

Factors are whole numbers which divide exactly into other numbers. Factors of 20 are {1, 2, 4, 5, 10, 20}

KEY FACTS 3

A **prime number** has only two factors: 1 and itself. Prime numbers up to 20 are: 2, 3, 5, 7, 11, 13, 17, 19

1 Read the question then read it again.

2 Study the numbers. — What are multiples of 4?

3 Look at the list of numbers. — Multiples of 4 are in the 4 times table:
4, 8, 12, 16, 20, 24, 28, 32, 36, 40, 44, 48, 52, 56...

4 Check the numbers then write the answers in the box. — Match the 4 times table with the numbers in the question 12, 15, 4, 48, 33, 13

5 Answer the question. — 4, 12, 48

Practice Questions

Look at the numbers in the cloud and use them to answer these questions:

13, 36, 4, 25, 1, 15, 18, 12, 37, 7, 28, 24

a) multiples of 6 ☐

b) prime numbers ☐

c) factors of 15 ☐

TOP TIP

When finding the factor of a number, remember

★ 1 is a factor of every number
★ The number itself is always a factor

Checking your answers

Inverse operations

Remember, adding and subtracting are OPPOSITES. Multiplying and dividing are OPPOSITES. We can use this knowledge to check our calculations quickly.

e.g.	$54 + 66 = 120$	CHECK	$120 - 54 = 66$
or	$56 \times 8 = 448$	CHECK	$448 \div 8 = 56$

INVERSE means the same as OPPOSITE

Question: $2028 \div 26 =$ ☐

1 Read the question then read it again.

Divide 2028 by 26.

2 Study the numbers. Picture them in your head.

Picture them on a number line.

3 Perform the calculation.

```
        78
  26 ⟌ 2028
       182
       208
```

4 Does the answer look sensible? If it does, check it using the INVERSE OPERATION.

The opposite of dividing is multiplying so...

```
     78
   x 26
    468
   1560
   2028
```

5 Does the check answer match the original sum? If it does, enter the answer in the box! If it doesn't, go back to Step 1.

Yes! Our answer is correct!

Practice Questions

Do these calculations and then check your answers using the inverse operation.

1) $87 \times 42 =$ ☐

2) $962 + 827 =$ ☐

3) $2268 \div 27 =$ ☐

4) $9047 - 582 =$ ☐

TOP TIP Get into the habit of checking your answers. It may help you do better in your test!

Rounding up or down

Another excellent way to check your answers is to round the numbers in the question up or down. Doing this will give you a simple sum to do and give you a rough answer.

Question: 42 x 38 = ☐

1 (Read the question then read it again.)   42 x 38 = ?

2 (Study the numbers.
Picture them in your head.)   Picture them on a number line.

3 (Perform the calculation.)

$$\begin{array}{r} 42 \\ \times\ \ 38 \\ \hline 336 \\ 1260 \\ \hline \mathbf{1596} \end{array}$$

4 (Now round off the numbers and
mentally calculate your answer.)

42 ROUND TO 40
38 ROUND TO 40
40 x 40 = 1600

5 (Are the answers reasonably close?
If so, enter your answer in the box.
If not, you must go back to Step 1.)

Yes, 1596 is pretty close to 1600.
Our answer looks correct!

Practice Questions

Do these calculations and then check your answers using the 'Rounding Up or Down' technique.

1) 92 × 68 = ☐

2) 4729 − 414 = ☐

3) 594 − 406 = ☐

4) 794 ÷ 19 = ☐

TOP TIP 1

When rounding up or down think of 'easy' numbers. These are numbers you can work with easily in your head. Some examples are 2, 5, 10, 50, 100 and so on.

TOP TIP 2

Get used to doing mental calculations every day. Give your brain 'gym exercises' to do which involve calculating numbers quickly. Darts can be a fun way to do this!

Multiplying and dividing by 10,100 and 1000

At Level 5 you must be able to multiply and divide whole numbers and decimals by 10, 100 and 1000.

Question: Write in the missing number.

5.23 x 10 = [ ]

1 Read the question then read it again.

5.23 x 10 =

2 Picture the numbers. What do they look like?

5.23 is nearly 5.

3 Study the numbers again and think about them.

You know the answer should be about 50 (5 x 10 = 50).

4 Remember the rules.

To multiply a decimal by 10 move the numbers one place to the left, leaving the decimal point in place.

5 Calculate.

5.23 x 10
Shift the numbers one place to the left.

6 Check your answer.

so 5.23 x 10 = 52.3
52.3 is nearly 50

7 If your answer looks sensible, write it in the box. If not, go back to Step 3.

From Step 3 we know our answer should be about 50. Our answer looks correct.

KEY FACTS

Multiplication
* To multiply a decimal by 100, move the numbers two places to the left.
* To multiply a decimal by 1000, move the numbers three places to the left.
* Sometimes you will need to add zeros to fill blank spaces.

e.g. $6.2 \times 100 = 620$
$2.71 \times 1000 = 2710$

TOP TIP

When multiplying whole numbers by 10, 100 and 1000, just add the correct number of zeros!

x 10   add 0 to the end   27 x 10 = 270

x 100   add 00 to the end   27 x 100 = 2700

x 1000 add 000 to the end   27 x 1000 = 27 000

Let's try another question. This time we will DIVIDE a decimal number.
(Remember: dividing is the opposite of multiplying.)

Question: Write in the missing number.

$79.6 \div 10 =$ ☐

1 (Read the question then read it again.) $79.6 \div 10 =$

2 (Picture the numbers. What do they look like?) 79.6 is nearly 80.

3 (Study the numbers again and think about them.) You know the answer should be about 8 $(80 \div 10 = 8)$.

4 (Remember the rules.) To divide a decimal by 10, move the numbers one place to the right.

5 (Calculate.) Shift the numbers one place to the right.

6 (Check your answer.) so $79.6 \div 10 = 7.96$
7.96 is nearly 8

7 (If your answer looks sensible, write it in the box. If not go back to Step 3.) From Step 3 we know our answer should be about 4. Our answer looks correct.

Practice Questions

1) $42 \times 10 =$ ☐

2) $87 \times$ ☐ $= 8700$

3) $0.9 \times 10 =$ ☐

4) $3.1 \div 10 =$ ☐

5) $596 \div$ ☐ $= 59.6$

6) $7200 \div 1000 =$ ☐

KEY FACTS

Division

★ To divide a decimal by 100, move the numbers **two** places to the right.

★ To divide a decimal by 1000, move the numbers **three** places to the right.

Decimals

To achieve Level 5 you must be able to work with numbers to two decimal places. Decimals are easy – remember, money is written with decimals! For example, £9.85 is nearly £10.00; 3.07 is a bit more than 3.

Question: Write in the missing number.

2.52 x 6.9 =

---

1 Read the question then read it again.

2.52 x 6.9 = ?

2 Picture the numbers. What do they look like?

2.52 is around halfway between 2 and 3. 6.9 is just less than 7.

3 Study the numbers again and think about them!

You know the answer is going to be more than 12 (2 x 6) and less than 21 (3 x 7). Remember there is a total of three numbers to the right of the decimal points.

4 When multiplying and dividing, remove the decimal point and calculate.

```
    252
  ×  69
   2268
  15120
  17388
```

5 Check back to your estimate at Step 3.

You know that your number is going to be between 12 and 21 (see Step 3).

6 Replace the decimal point.

Count three in from the right (see Step 3). Your answer is 17.388.

7 Round up or down so you only have 2 numbers after the decimal point.

17.388 becomes 17.39 when you round to two decimal places.

8 If your answer looks sensible, write it in the box.

If it doesn't look right, go back to Step 3 and try again.

TOP TIP 1

When rounding, remember 5 is always UP!

4.275 = 4.28

TOP TIP 2

When writing money remember:

£0.45p (✗) £0.45 (✔)
0.45p (✗) 45p (✔)

Say the answer to yourself before you write it down!

Question: (5.84 – 2.97) x 3 = [ ]

1 (Read the question then read it again.)   (5.84 - 2.97) x 3 = ?

2 (Picture the numbers. What do they look like?)   5.84 rounds to 6.
2.97 rounds to 3.

3 (Study the numbers again and think about them!)   6 - 3 = 3
3 x 3 = 9

4 (Calculate.)

Remember – always do the bits in brackets first.

i)		ii)	
	5.84		2.87
–	2.97	×	3
	2.87		8.61

5 (Check back to your estimate at Step 3.)   You know that your number is going to be around 9 (see Step 3 above).

6 (Make sure your decimal point is in the right place.)   Your answer is 8.61.

7 (Round up or down so you only have two numbers after the decimal point.)   You only have two numbers after the decimal point so you don't need to do anything.

8 (If your answer looks sensible, write it in the box.)   If it doesn't, go back to Step 3 and try again.

Practice Questions

Here are some questions for you to try. Remember to use the step-by-step approach above. Write your answers to two decimal places.

1) (4.6 + 2.75) × 3.21 = [ ]

2) £30 – (£4.52 × 4) = [ ]

3) (7.2 + 4.69) × 2.30 = [ ]

4) £42 – (£2.75 × 6) = [ ]

TOP TIP 1

B - Brackets

O - Powers

D - Division

M - Multiplication

A - Addition

S - Subtraction

This shows the order in which calculations must be done: brackets should be done first then powers, then division, etc

Reducing fractions

Reducing fractions is all about finding a fraction's 'common factors'.
For example:

$\frac{4}{6}$ can be reduced to $\frac{2}{3}$ (because 4 and 6 can both be divided by 2)

$\frac{2}{4}$ can be reduced to $\frac{1}{2}$ (because 2 and 4 can both be divided by 2)

Question: What is $\frac{54}{126}$ in its lowest form?

---

1 Read the question then read it again.

2 Are both numbers divisible by 2?
Yes? Then divide them both by 2.
No? Move to Step 4.

Yes $54 \div 2 = 27$
       $126 \div 2 = 63$

3 Look at your new fraction.
Can the numbers be divided by 2 again?
Yes? Repeat Step 2.
No? Move to Step 4.

$\frac{27}{63}$

Both numbers cannot be divided by 2
so we move to Step 4.

4 Study the fraction. Which number
(other than 1) can be divided into
both the top and bottom numbers?

Both 27 and 63 can be divided by 9!

5 Reduce the fraction.
Enter your answer in the box.

$27 \div 9 = 3$ $63 \div 9 = 7$

Our answer is $\frac{3}{7}$

Practice Questions

Reduce each of these fractions to their lowest form.

1) $\frac{48}{64} = $ ☐   2) $\frac{15}{45} = $ ☐   3) $\frac{42}{49} = $ ☐   4) $\frac{21}{24} = $ ☐

TOP TIP 1 Learn to recognise these

equivalent fractions.

$\frac{1}{3} = \frac{2}{6} = \frac{3}{9} = \frac{4}{12} = \frac{5}{15} = \frac{6}{18} = \frac{7}{21}$

$\frac{1}{4} = \frac{2}{8} = \frac{3}{12} = \frac{4}{16} = \frac{5}{20} = \frac{6}{24} = \frac{7}{28}$

$\frac{1}{5} = \frac{2}{10} = \frac{3}{15} = \frac{4}{20} = \frac{5}{25} = \frac{6}{30} = \frac{7}{35}$

TOP TIP 2

Remember, when you are reducing a fraction
ask yourself the following questions before
writing anything down:

★ Which numbers fit?
★ How many times do they fit?

You can use your ability to reduce fractions to their lowest form to help you answer questions on RATIO and PROPORTION.

Question: Look at this pattern of squares:

What is the ratio of blue squares to white squares?

1 Read the question then read it again.

2 Count the number of blue squares.   There are 4 blue squares.

3 Now count the white squares.   There are 8 white squares.

4 What is the ratio of blue squares to white squares?   The ratio is 4:8

5 Can you reduce the ratio?   Follow Step 2 to Step 5 on page 20.

6 Write your answer in the box.   Write this as a ratio 1:2

KEY FACTS

When doing a question about proportion, count the TOTAL number of squares. This can be written as a fraction.

The proportion of blue squares in the pattern at the top of this page is 4 in 12 or $\frac{4}{12}$.
Reduce this using the steps on page 20. The proportion of blue squares in the whole pattern is 1 in 3 or $\frac{1}{3}$.

Practice Questions

Look at the pattern below and answer the following questions:

1) What is the ratio of blue counters to white counters?

2) What is the proportion of white counters in the whole pattern?

TOP TIP If you are asked to find a **proportion** of two things or numbers you are being asked to find a **fraction** (in its lowest form).

Calculating fractions or percentages

Without a calculator

Lots of questions that ask you to find fractions or percentages of things are easy to answer WITHOUT a calculator by just using some simple techniques, such as doubling, halving or dividing by 10. For example:

70% of 900 metres	10% of 900 is 90	
so	70% of 900 is 7 x 90	
	7 x 90 = 630	= 630 metres

Question: A CD player costs £150. Tim's dad pays 35% of the cost.

How much is left for Tim to pay? [   ]

1 Read the question then read it again. What am I being asked to do?

You need to find the amount Tim has to pay.

2 To find the amount, first calculate 10% of the original price.

10% of £150 = £15.

3 Now calculate 5% of the original price and add your answers together to find 35%.

5% is half of 10% so 5% is £7.50.
10% + 10% + 10% + 5% = 35%
£15 + £15 + £15 + £7.50 = £52.50

4 Don't forget the next part. How much is left for Tim to pay?

Tim's dad pays £52.50.
So Tim has to pay £150 - £52.50 = £97.50

5 Check you have answered the question properly.

How much does Tim have to pay?
After his dad has paid £52.50 he has to pay £97.50.

TOP TIP 1

These are some shortcuts you may find helpful:

a) To find 1% of something, first find 10% then find 10% of THAT answer. You can work out any % by adding all the 10%, 5% and 1% answers together!

b) You can also subtract to find a percentage. For example, 99% could be worked out by working out 1% of the total and subtracting from 100%.

TOP TIP 2

Remember as many percentage/fraction equivalents as you can:

$50\% = \frac{1}{2}$ $25\% = \frac{1}{4}$ $75\% = \frac{3}{4}$

$33\% =$ nearly $\frac{1}{3}$ $66\% =$ nearly $\frac{2}{3}$

You can work out many fractions or percentages very easily without a calculator but sometimes it's not so easy. For example, if you scored 15 out of 30 in your maths test you should be able to recognise that you got 50% correct. If you improved the following week and got 24 out of 30 then you may need to use your calculator. Calculate as follows:

Key in **24** then **÷** then **30** then **%**

You should have the answer 80, which means you scored 80% correct.

You also need to be able to work out fractions of a quantity. The word 'of' means multiply.

Question: Work $\frac{3}{5}$ of £120 [ ]

1 (Read the question then read it again.)   Find $\frac{3}{5}$ of 120.

2 (Work out what $\frac{1}{5}$ is worth.) $\frac{1}{5}$ x 120. This is the same as dividing 120 by 5.
120 ÷ 5 = 24.

3 (Work out what $\frac{3}{5}$ is worth.)   If $\frac{1}{5}$ = 24 then multiply by 3 to find $\frac{3}{5}$. 3 x 24 = 72.

4 (Add in the units.)   £72

5 (Check that the answer sounds sensible and write it in the answer box.)

Practice Questions 1

Work these out without a calculator:

1) 25% of £400 [ ]   2) 15% of 180 cm [ ]   3) 45% of 60 g [ ]

4) 70% of 1100 ml [ ]   5) 55% of 170 km [ ]   6) 40% of 210 cm [ ]

Practice Questions 2

Work these out without a calculator:

1) $\frac{5}{6}$ of £30 [ ]   3) $\frac{3}{4}$ of 84 g [ ]

2) $\frac{5}{7}$ of 77 ml [ ]   4) $\frac{7}{9}$ of 72 m [ ]

Multiplication and division

To get a Level 5 you need to be able to multiply and divide a 3-digit number by a 2-digit number without a calculator! EASY!

Question: Write in the missing number. 415 x 49 = [   ]

1 Read the question then read it again. | 415 x 49 =

2 Picture the numbers. | 415 is close to 400.
49 is close to 50.

3 Study the numbers and think about them. | 415 x 49 is approximately
400 x 50 = 20000

4 Calculate your answer.

```
      415
   x   49
     3735   (415 x 9)
    16600   (415 x 40)
    20335
```

5 Does your answer look sensible? If it does then write it in the box. If it doesn't then go back to Step 3. | 20335 is close to 20000 (see Step 3). Our answer looks sensible!

Write in the missing number. 587 x 32 = [   ]

1 Read the question then read it again. | 587 x 32 =

2 Picture the numbers. | 587 is close to 600.
32 is close to 30.

3 Study the numbers and think about them. | 587 x 32 is approximately
600 x 30 = 18 000

4 Calculate your answer.

```
      587
   x   32
     1174   (587 x 2)
    17610   (587 x 30)
    18784
```

5 Does your answer look sensible? If it does, write it in the box. If it doesn't, go back to Step 3. | 18784 is approximately 18000 (see Step 3). Our answer looks sensible!

Now let's try division. Write in the missing number. 978 ÷ 15 = [   ]

1 (Read the question then read it again.)   978 ÷ 15 =

2 (Picture the numbers – what do they look like?)   978 rounds to 1000.
15 rounds to 20.

3 (Study the numbers and think about them.)   978 ÷ 15 is approximately
1000 ÷ 20 = 50

4 (Calculate your answer.)

$$\begin{array}{r} 65.2 \\ 15\overline{)978} \\ 90 \\ \hline 78 \\ -75 \\ \hline 30 \\ -30 \\ \hline 00 \end{array}$$

5 (If your answer looks sensible, write it in the box.)   Our answer (to one decimal place) is 65.2.

Practice Questions Try these for practice.

1) 351 ÷ 27 = [   ]

2) 221 ÷ 17 [   ]

3) 432 ÷ [   ] = 27

4) 271 × 42 = [   ]

5) 784 × 83 = [   ]

6) 225 × [   ] = 8100

KEY FACTS x and ÷ are opposites

Use this fact to help with tricky questions. For example:

21 x 16 = 336   336 ÷ 21 = 16
16 x [   ] = 336   so   336 ÷ 16 = 21   Our missing number is 21.

TOP TIP

If you find the traditional way of doing long multiplication difficult, use the grid method.

271 x 52

	200	70	1
50	10000	3500	50
2	400	140	2
	10400	3640	52

= 14092

TOP TIP

Be neat. Keep your numbers in the right columns.

WRONG ✗	RIGHT ✓
312	312
x 14	x 14
3120	3120
1248	1248
4368	4368

Negative numbers

NEGATIVE NUMBERS ARE EASY. Imagine a thermometer and you have a number line with positive and negative numbers.

-7 is a negative number.
7 is a positive number – we do not need to put in the positive sign.

Question: Put these temperatures in order from coldest to warmest:

53°, −24°, 23°, 3°, −20°, 0°, −25°

---

1 Read the question then read it again.

Remember, negative numbers are colder than positive numbers, so an increase in temperature is a movement right on the number line or up on a thermometer.

2 Picture the numbers.

Group the numbers.
Negative: (−24°, −20°, −25°)
Positive: (53°, 23°, 3°, 0°)

3 Study the numbers.

Draw a number line. Don't forget to include 'zero'. Decide where each number goes.

-25° -24° -20°　　　0° 3°　　　23°　　　　53°

4 Check your answer.

Are the numbers in order?
Check you have used every number.

5 If your answer looks sensible, write it in the box.

If not go back to Step 3 and try again.

TOP TIP 1

Numbers are often called INTEGERS. Don't let this put you off. This just means WHOLE numbers without decimals.

These are integers　　　1, 2, 3, 4
These are not integers　　5.6, 7.8, 11.3

TOP TIP 2

When thinking of negative (−) numbers, think of a ladder going into a hole in the ground.

-2 is higher than -6
-2 is a larger number than -6
-5 is below -4
-5 is a smaller number than -4

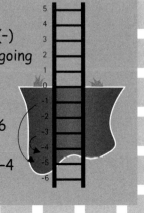

Question: The temperature is −8°. It rises by 11°.

What is the new temperature?

---

1 (Read the question then read it again.) Rises means getting warmer.

2 (Picture the numbers.) −8° is colder than 11°.

3 (Calculate your answer.)

−9 −8 −7 −6 −5 −4 −3 −2 −1 0 1 2 3 4 5 6 7 8 9 10

The temperature starts at -8°.
We then need to count up 11 places.

4 (Check your answer.) Did you count in the right direction? When adding to a negative number always count to the right on a number line.

5 (If your answer checks out, write it in the box.) Our answer is 3° which is 11° warmer than −8°!

−25 −24 −23 −22 −21 −20 −19 −18 −17 −16 −15 −14 −13 −12 −11 −10 −9 −8 −7 −6 −5 −4 −3 −2 −1 −0 1 2 3 4 5 6 7 8 9 10 11 12 13 14 15 16 17 18 19 20 21 22 23 24 25

Practice Questions

Use the number line to help you.

1) Put these temperatures in order, lowest to highest:

−6°, 4°, 0°, −2°, 3°

[ ] [ ] [ ] [ ] [ ]

2) Order these numbers correctly starting with the smallest:

−46, 27, 18, −31, −33

[ ] [ ] [ ] [ ] [ ]

3) The temperature in a new freezer is 20°C. When the freezer is switched on the temperature falls by 6°C every hour. How many hours until it has reached -10°C. [ ]

4) On Tuesday the temperature was −7°. On Wednesday the temperature was 13°. What is the difference between Tuesday's and Wednesday's temperatures? [ ]

Simple formulae

Formulae can be written in words or in letters. To achieve Level 5 you may be required to make up your own formulae in the tests. This is easier than it sounds! Let's start by working through this example.

Question: Here is a formula for finding the total weight of some bags of equipment.

$$W = 200g \times N$$

W = total weight
200g is the weight of each bag
N is the number of bags

Now write the formula for the weight of one bag if N bags weigh 900g and one bag weighs B.

1 Read the question then read it again.

Lots to read and think about here!

2 What am I being asked to do?

You need to write a formula for the weight of one bag using 900g and B.

3 It will help if you say the formula to yourself.

The total weight is the weight of one bag (B) multiplied by the total number of bags (N).
So...
The weight of one bag is the total weight (900g) divided by the total number of bags.

4 Change your logical statement into a simple formula. Say it to yourself when you write it down.

The weight of one bag   B
    ...is the total weight...   900g
    ...divided by the total number of boxes   N

5 Does your answer look correct?

$$B = 900 \div N \quad \text{OR} \quad B = \frac{900}{N}$$

TOP TIP 1

★ Talk through your formula in your head.
★ Think clearly.
★ Take it step by step.

TOP TIP 2

It helps to only use letters that relate to the information in the question, e.g. C = Cost.

A simple formula is often used to find out the total cost of items bought.
In words this formula can be written:

"The total cost is the price of one item multiplied by the number of those items bought."

In letter formulae this could be written as: T = N x P

T = total cost   P = price of each item   N = number of items bought

Practice Questions 1

Use the T = P × N formula to work out these questions.

1) What is the value of T if N = 12 and P = £8?

2) What is the value of N if T = £50 and P = £12.50?

3) What is the value of P if T = £48 and N = 3?

Example question

A cabinet maker works out the length of a cupboard by multiplying the width by 2 and adding 5.
Write a formula to show the process the cabinet maker goes through to get his answer.
Use L for the length and W for the width.

L = $(W \times 2) + 5 = 2W + 5$

Practice Question 2

To calculate the length of a bookcase he multiplies the width by 5 and adds 12.
Write a formula to show the process the cabinet maker goes through to get his answer.
Use L for length and W for width.

L =

TOP TIP 3

If a number and a letter are next to each other, e.g. 4N, it means they are multiplied.
Why is the x (multiply) symbol left out? It could get confused with the letter x!!

Understanding and simplifying expressions

Expressions are easy to use but remember:

★ Letters are used to represent numbers.

★ Simplify means 'put like terms together'.

Question: Amy has *n* beads. Write down an expression that shows how many beads each student has using *n*.

a) Robert has three times as many beads as Amy.
b) Imran has four less beads than Amy.
c) Molly has five more beads than Robert.

1 (Read the question then read it again.)   You need to write 3 expressions. These do not have equals signs but will include *n*.

2 (Look at the numbers and the letters.)   Amy has *n* beads. Robert has 3 times as many, so that's 3 × *n*. Imran has 4 less, that's –4. Molly has 5 more than Robert, that's +5.

3 (Write the expressions as you say it.)   a) *Robert has 3 × n or 3n beads.*
b) *Imran has n - 4 beads.*
c) *Molly has 3n + 5 beads.*

4 (Check the answer.)

TOP TIP

Symbols are used in special ways.

$a + a = 2a$

$c \times d = cd$

$a \times b \times 2 = 2ab$

$p \times p = p2$

$a \div b = \dfrac{a}{b}$

KEY FACTS

Remember these important terms:

Expression – this is a mixture of letters, symbols and numbers.

Formula – formulae are about finding out. If you can use the variables you know how to work out the missing one,

ie: $v = u + at.$ If $u = 10$, $a = 2$, $t = 5$

Then $v = 10 + 5 \times 2$

$v = 20$

Equation – this must have an equals sign. It has an unknown value which you need to work out.

Simplifying expressions

When you have expressions that have some of the same terms, you can simplify them by collecting like terms. Like terms have the same letters and powers.

Question: Simplify the following expression:

$$3a + 6b - a + 2b - a$$

1 (Read the question then read it again.)   I need to simplify the expression.

2 (Look at the numbers and letters.)   There are a's and b's. The answer will include an 'a' term and a 'b' term.

3 (Group the terms to make the expression simpler.) $3a - a - a + 6b + 2b$

4 (Simplify.) $3a - a - a + 6b + 2b = a + 8b$

5 (Check the answer.)   The expression has an 'a' term and a 'b' term.

Practice Questions

1). Simplify these expressions

a) $5a + 2a - b$ b) $2a + 5b - b - 6a$ c) $4m + 3m - 2m + 6n - 5n$

2). John is y years old.
     Sara is two years older than John.
     Kate is five years younger than John.
     Alfie is twice as old as John.

Write an expression in terms of y for each of their ages.

Name	Age
John	
Sara	
Kate	
Alfie	

Coordinates

To achieve Level 5 you should be familiar with coordinates and quadrants.

Let's try a question to practise what we know!

Question: Write down the coordinates of each point on this graph.

1st quadrant = (_ , _)

2nd quadrant = (_ , _)

3rd quadrant = (_ , _)

4th quadrant = (_ , _)

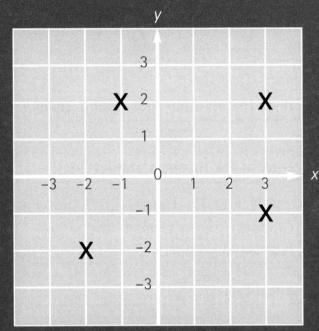

Remember which quadrant is which!

2nd	1st
3rd	4th

1 Read the question then read it again.

2 Practise your answer.

You can sketch in lines to help you read the coordinates.

3 Check the number of each quadrant.

2nd quadrant	y	1st quadrant
3rd quadrant		4th quadrant

→x

4 Read off the coordinates in each quadrant.z

Remember:
ALONG the x axis first then UP or DOWN the y axis

1 (3, 2)   2 (−1, 2)
3 (−2, −2)   4 (3, −1)

5 Double-check and write in your answer.

Check twice! Write once!

Let's try another question.

Draw a reflection of the pentagon in the x axis. Record the coordinates of each vertex.

(__ , __)
(__ , __)
(__ , __)
(__ , __)
(__ , __)

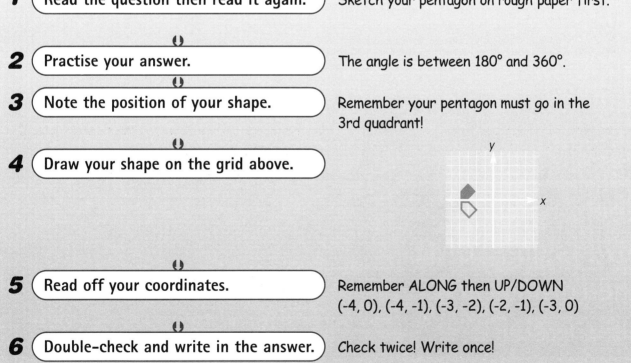

1 (Read the question then read it again.)   Sketch your pentagon on rough paper first.

2 (Practise your answer.)   The angle is between 180° and 360°.

3 (Note the position of your shape.)   Remember your pentagon must go in the 3rd quadrant!

4 (Draw your shape on the grid above.)

5 (Read off your coordinates.)   Remember ALONG then UP/DOWN
(-4, 0), (-4, -1), (-3, -2), (-2, -1), (-3, 0)

6 (Double-check and write in the answer.)   Check twice! Write once!

When you feel comfortable with this,
try the practice questions over the page...

Practice Questions

1 In which quadrants will
   we find:

   (–4, –3)?   (–5, 3)?   (3, 2)?

   [ ]   [ ]   [ ]

   Now plot each coordinate

2 Draw a reflection of the
   parallelogram in the x axis. Name
   the coordinates of the reflected
   shape.

   (__, __) (__, __) (__, __) (__, __)

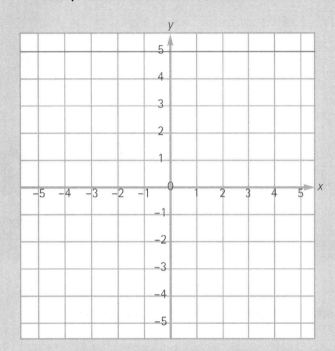

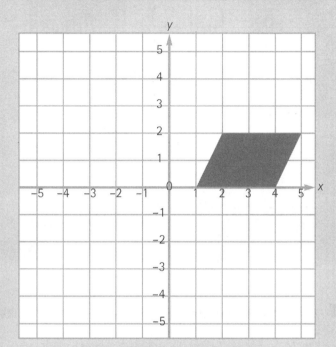

TOP TIP 1

This can help you to remember how
to read coordinates:

> ### Coordinates always go ALONG the corridor and UP the stairs.

Always go along first when reading
coordinates. x (axis) comes before y (axis)!

TOP TIP 2

Coordinates are always written in brackets
with a comma in between.

(3, 4) (–3, –2) or (x axis, y axis)

TOP TIP 3

The coordinates plot where the grid lines
cross, not the space in between them.

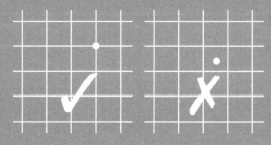

Angles

To achieve Level 5 you will need to be able to measure and draw angles and use the correct language for them. You must measure and draw angles accurately to within two degrees, otherwise you do not get the mark.

Measuring angles   Use an angle measurer or a protractor to measure these angles.

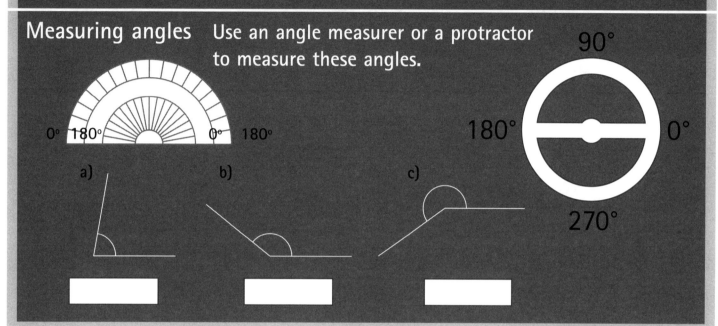

a)   b)   c)

---

1 (Read the question then read it again.)

We need to work out the angles.

2 (Use the curved line to help you find the angle you need to measure.)

Where will you measure? Use the curved line to help you.

3 (Study the angles.)

Estimate and label the angles to help you check your answers:
(a) is an acute angle – less than 90°.
(b) is an obtuse angle – more than 90° and less than 180°.
(c) is a reflex angle – more than 180° and less than 360°.

4 (Measure the angles.)

Match up the angle measurer and the lines carefully.

5 (Check your answers against your estimates in Step 3.)

Does each answer match your estimate?

6 (If your answer looks sensible, write it in the box.)

If not, go back to Step 3 and try again.

Drawing angles

Let's try drawing some angles. Use some paper to practise.

Question: Use an angle measurer or a protractor to draw these angles to the nearest degree.

(a) 47°   (b) 73°   (c) 164°

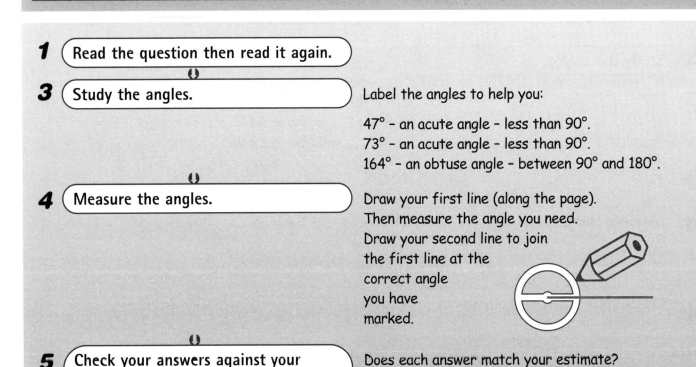

1 (Read the question then read it again.)

3 (Study the angles.)   Label the angles to help you:

47° – an acute angle – less than 90°.
73° – an acute angle – less than 90°.
164° – an obtuse angle – between 90° and 180°.

4 (Measure the angles.)   Draw your first line (along the page).
Then measure the angle you need.
Draw your second line to join
the first line at the
correct angle
you have
marked.

5 (Check your answers against your estimates in Step 2.)   Does each answer match your estimate?

To achieve Level 5 you also need to be able to measure or work out the size of the angles in a triangle and at a point.

Just remember: angles in a triangle add up to 180°.

Question: Find the missing angles in these triangles.

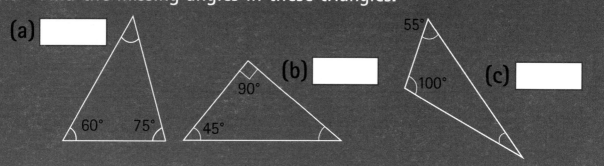

(a)

(b)

(c)

55°

100°

90°

60° 75°

45°

1 (Read the question then read it again.)

We are given two angles. We need to work out the missing angle.

2 (Picture the shape and remember the formula.)

Angles in a triangle add up to 180°.

3 (Study the numbers.)

You know two angles so you can work out the third.

4 (Calculate your answer.)

60° + 75° = 135°
180° − 135° = 45°

5 (Check your answer.)

Add the three angles together:
60° + 75° + 45° = 180°

6 (If your answer checks out, write it in the box.)

If not, return to Step 3.

Can you work out the remaining two missing angles?

TOP TIP 1

Always turn the paper to make the angles easier to measure.

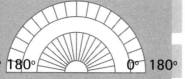

0° 180°   0° 180°

Keep your measurer straight!

Make sure you read the correct scale.

TOP TIP 2

Remember that the angles in a triangle and the angles on a straight line always add up to 180°.

Angles at a point

Question: Calculate the angle at this point.

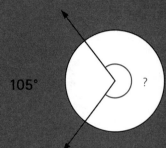

105°

1 (Read the question then read it again.) Calculate usually means you need to do a sum to work out the answer!

2 (Picture the shape. Estimate the angle.) The angle is between 180° and 360°.

3 (Remember the formula.) A complete turn = 360°

4 (Study the numbers.) You know one angle so you can work out the other.

5 (Calculate your answer.) 360° – 105° = 225°

6 (Check your answer.) Does it match your estimate?

7 (If your answer checks out, write it in the box.) If not, return to Step 4.

TOP TIP 1

A complete turn = 360°

So angles at a point add up to 360°

Imagine a skateboarder turning right around.

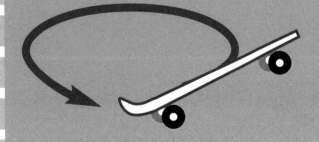

TOP TIP 2

A right angle is always shown by a box.

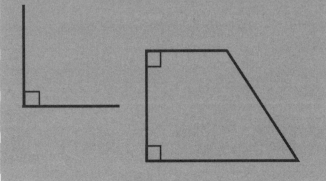

Practice Questions

1) Find the missing angles in these triangles.

(a)

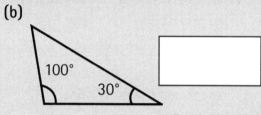

(b)

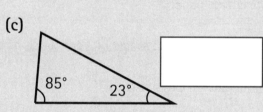

(c)

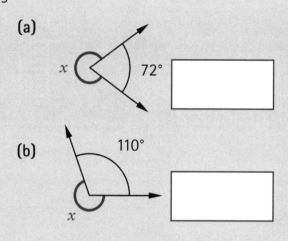

2) Find the angle labelled x in the diagrams below:

(a)

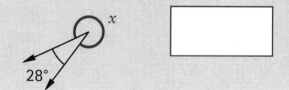

(b)

(c)

3) Estimate the size of these angles. Then label them acute, reflex, obtuse or right angled.

(a)   (b)

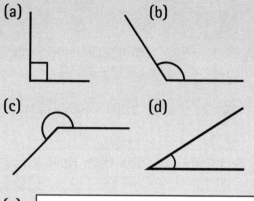

(c)   (d)

(a)

(b)

(c)

(d)

4) Draw an angle of 85° to the nearest degree.

5) Measure this angle to the nearest degree.

Reflection, rotation and translation

To achieve Level 5 in Maths you will need to understand reflection, rotation and translation.

Question: Draw the reflection of this shape in the mirror line.

REFLECTION
An image of an object or shape
on the other side of a mirror line.

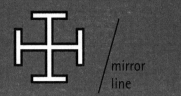

mirror line

1 (Read the question then read it again.)

2 (Practise your answer.)   Trace the shape and the mirror line onto practice paper.

3 (Now complete the reflection.)   Draw in the reflected shape on your piece of paper.

4 (Test your answer.)   Fold your paper. Does it work?

5 (If it looks right, draw in your answer.)   If not, go back to Step 3.

Question: Does this shape have rotational symmetry?

ROTATIONAL SYMMETRY
When a shape appears the same as it is rotated.

1 (Read the question then read it again.)

2 (Practise your answer.)   Trace the shape.

3 (Test your answer.)   Rotate the shape 360°. Does the shape look the same in any other position?

| 0° | 90° | 180° | 270° |

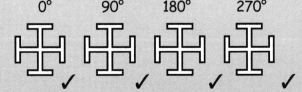

4 (Check your answer and write it in.)   Yes. The shape looks the same as it does at the start when it is turned around 360 degrees! The shape does have rotational symmetry, of order 4.

Let's try a question about translation now.

Sketch the position of the shape after a translation of 3 squares right and 4 squares down.

TRANSLATION
A movement of a shape from one point to another. Size and shape do not change.

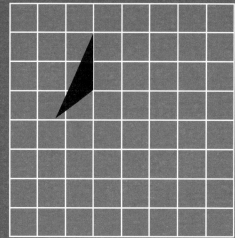

1 (Read the question then read it again.)   'translation' = slide along.

2 (Practise your answer.)   Trace the shape and practise before you write in your answer.

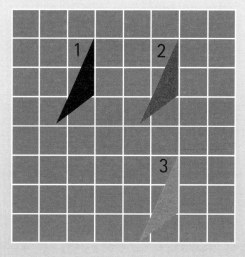

3 (Draw in your final answer.)   Double-check first.

TOP TIP 1

The order of rotational symmetry is the number of times the shape turns but still looks the same.

TOP TIP 2

When a shape is translated, reflected or rotated it is still the size size or shape. This image is therefore congruent to the original shape.

Practice Questions

1) Draw the reflections of these shapes.

(a)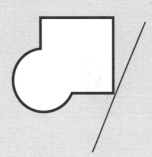

(b)

(c)

(d)

(e)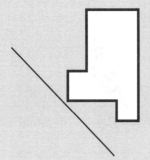

(f)

2) Which of these shapes have rotational symmetry?
   Tick those that do and write down the order of rotational symmetry.

(a)

(b)

(c)

(d)

Practice Questions

3) Tick the correctly translated shapes, and describe the translation from shape A to shape B.

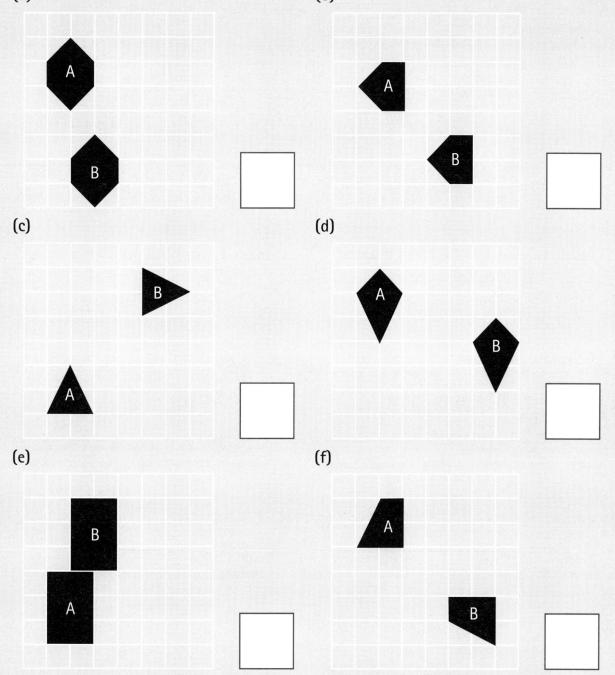

(a)

(b)

(c)

(d)

(e)

(f)

TOP TIP 1

Lines of symmetry = Mirror lines.

The image is the same distance from the mirror line as the object is in front of it.

TOP TIP 2

Don't let your paper slip!

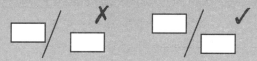

Units of measure

Comparing metric to imperial units of measure

To achieve Level 5 you will have to answer questions that ask you to compare metric units of measurement (kilometres, grams, litres and centimetres) with imperial units of measurement (miles, pounds, pints).

Question: Sue needs 2 pounds of fruit to make a jar of jam.
How many kilograms should she buy to make 11 jars of jam?

---

1 (Read the question then read it again.)   2 pounds x 11 jars = how many kilograms is this?

2 (Study the units.)   She needs 22 pounds of fruit.
$1lb = \frac{5}{11}$ kg

3 (Calculate the answer.) $22 \times \frac{5}{11} = 10$

4 (Remember the units you need for the answer.)   The answer is 10kg

---

Practice Questions

Here are some questions. Use the Key Facts on page 59 to help you.

1) A water urn will hold 10 litres of water.
   How many **pints** is this?

   [   ] pints

2) Lai drives 35 miles.
   How many **kilometres** has he driven?

   [   ] kilometres

TOP TIP 1

Revision rhymes!

> A metre is just 3 feet 3.
> It's longer than a yard you see!
> 2 and a bit pounds of jam is
> round about 1 kilo of ham!

To achieve Level 5 you will have to answer questions that ask you to convert one metric unit to another metric unit.

Question: Write 8250 ml as litres.

1 (Read the question then read it again.)   8250 ml = ? litres

2 (Study the units.)   1 litre = 1000 ml

3 (Calculate the answer.)   8250 ÷ 1000 = 8.25

4 (Add in the correct units.)   8.25 litres

5 (If your answer looks sensible, it in the box.)   If not, go back to Step 2 and try again.

Practice Questions
Try some more questions.

1) My water bottle holds 150cl.
   How many millilitres does it hold?

2) If I removed 1820kg of stone from one wall and 2150kg from another wall how much stone did I remove altogether?

   Circle the correct answer.

   (a) 39.7 tonnes
   (b) 3.97 tonnes
   (c) 0.397 tonnes

3) An electrician has a wire that is 1.5km long.
   How many 4m lengths can be cut from it?

TOP TIP 2
Make up some of your own questions to help you to compare units.

What would you prefer, 1 litre or 1000 ml of cola?

TOP TIP 3
Measure things around you to get a feel for the different units.

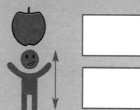

g   or   kg

m

Estimating measures

To achieve Level 5 you will have to estimate measures accurately. This mainly involves using common sense though, so don't worry. You will just need to think about length, weight and quantity in different amounts. These three questions are examples. The notes should help you with estimating.

LENGTH
Suggest things you would measure in kilometres, metres, centimetres and millimetres.

★ **Kilometres** Anything or anywhere that is too far to walk! For example: the distance to the moon.

★ **Metres** Anything or anywhere that you could walk to or around. For example: the garden, playground or bedroom.

★ **Centimetres** Anything you could step over. For example: books, TVs or cereal packets.

★ **Millimetres** Anything you could step on and squash! For example: ants, Smarties or peanuts.

MASS
Suggest things you would measure in tonnes, kilograms and grams.

★ **Tonnes** Anything you and your friends couldn't lift. For example: a ship, an aeroplane or an elephant!

★ **Kilograms** Anything you and an adult could lift. For example: a table, your friend, the sofa.

★ **Grams** Anything you could hold in the palm of your hand. For example: a gerbil, a tennis ball.

CAPACITY
Suggest things you would measure in litres, centilitres and millilitres.

★ **Litres** Anything that is too much for you to drink. For example: the bath, a swimming pool.

★ **Centilitres** Anything you might drink if you were thirsty. For example: a mug of tea, a glass of milk.

★ **Millilitres** Anything that is just a mouthful. For example: a teaspoon of medicine, a sachet of ketchup.

TOP TIP

Get used to thinking about measures and remember a few standard ones to compare against others.

100 m = the length of a football pitch
1 kg = a bag of sugar
1 litre = a carton of juice

Then think about these:

50 m = $\frac{1}{2}$ the length of a football pitch
20 kg = 20 bags of sugar
100 litres = 100 cartons of juice

Picture them in your head.

Practice Questions

1) Estimate the lengths of the following items. Then measure them.
   Include the unit of measurement you are using.

Item	Estimated length (with unit)	Actual length (with unit)
(a) Your maths book		
(b) Your table		
(c) Your classroom		
(d) Your sports hall		

2) Which unit of measurement would you use to measure the following?

(a) The weight of a toaster

(b) The distance from Paris to Rome

(c) The amount of water in a swimming pool

(d) The weight of a cereal bar

(e) The length of a baked bean

(f) The amount of milk in a bottle

(g) The weight of a caravan

(h) The length of a football pitch

(i) The amount of juice squeezed from a lemon

KEY FACTS - MEASURE

You may come across a question such as this.

Question: Suggest how you could measure the thickness of one sheet of paper.

This question is trying to catch you out but don't worry! All you have to do is to measure a large pile of paper and divide the total thickness by the number of pieces of paper in the pile.

So...

100 sheets of paper = 75 mm thick

75 ÷ 100 = 0.75 mm

Each sheet of paper is 0.75 mm thick

The area of a rectangle

There is an easy way to remember how to answer questions about the area of rectangles. Just remember this formula:

Area of a rectangle = the length x the width.

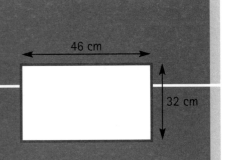

46 cm

32 cm

Question: Find the area of this rectangle.

---

1 (Read the question then read it again.)

TAKE NOTE: you are working with AREA, so you need a formula!

2 (Remember your formula.)

The area of a rectangle = the length x the width.

3 (Picture the numbers. What do they look like?)

32 cm is almost 30 cm. 46 cm is almost 50 cm Use this to estimate the answer.

4 (Study the numbers again and think about them.)

You can estimate that the answer should be around 1500 (50 x 30 = 1500).

5 (Calculate your answer.)

```
      46
  x   32
      92
    1380
    1472
```

6 (Add in your unit of measurement.)

cm squared (cm²)   1472 cm²

7 (Check your answer against your estimate in Step 4.)

1472 is close to 1500.

8 (If your answer looks sensible, write it in the box.)

If not, go back to Step 4 and try again.

TOP TIP 1

When dealing with area, make sure the units are ALWAYS squared.

e.g.   cm²   m²   km²

TOP TIP 2

Break up complicated shapes into smaller rectangles to make the question easier to answer. Remember to add up the areas of all the rectangles to get your answer!

Let's try another question. Here is a shape you will have to divide up into smaller shapes.

Find the area of this shape.

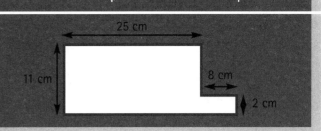

1 (Read the question then read it again.)   Look for the key words: area and shape.

2 (Picture the shape.)   It looks like two rectangles joined together!

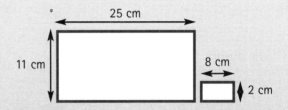

3 (Remember the formula.)   The area of a rectangle = the length x the width.
We need to measure two rectangles.

4 (Find the areas of the two rectangles.
Then add them together.)

25 x 11 = 275
8 x 2 = 16
Total = 291

5 (Add in your unit of measurement.)   291 cm²

6 (If your answer looks sensible,
write it in the box.)   If not, go back to Step 4 and try again.

Practice Questions
Try some more questions.

1) Find the area of this shape.

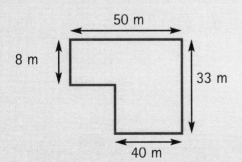

2) Find the area of this shape.

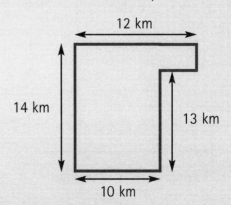

Finding the mean

Mean data is not 'nasty data'! You will need to be able to find the mean of a group of figures to achieve Level 5. Let's try a question.

Just remember: mean = average.

Question: Find the mean of these weights.

25 g   64 g   175 g   53 g   113 g

1 (Read the question then read it again.)   'mean' = average

2 (Think about the question.)   Mean – add up the group of numbers and divide by how many numbers there are in the group.

3 (Study the numbers.)   Your answer will be less than 175 g (the heaviest) and more than 25 g (the lightest). There are 5 different weights.

4 (Calculate your answer.)   25 + 64 + 175 + 53 + 113 = 430
430 ÷ 5 = 86

5 (Add in the unit of measurement.)   86 g

6 (If your answer looks sensible, write it in the box.)   If not, go back to Step 3 and try again.

Practice Questions

Find the mean of these sets of numbers.

1) 6, 2, 9, 6, 5, 4

2) 87, 89, 99, 91

3) 26, 19, 32, 27, 14, 21

4) 2.7, 4.6, 3.8, 2.9

TOP TIP 1

To find the mean:
Remember to add up all the values and divide by the number of values.

TOP TIP 2

If using a calculator, the  button must be pressed before dividing by the number of values.

Finding the median

Just remember median is the middle number in a group, when the numbers are placed in order of size.

Question: Look at these times and find the median.

23 secs,   64 secs,   24 secs,   42.4 secs,   42.04 secs

The median number is

1 Read the question then read it again.

2 Think about the question.

Median is the middle number in the group.

3 Picture the numbers.

Put them in order from lowest to highest:
23, 24, 42.02, 42.4, 64

4 Study the numbers and work out the answer.

42.04 is the middle number in this set of numbers.

5 Add in the unit of measurement.

42.04 secs

6 If your answer looks sensible, write it in the box.

If not, go back to Step 4 and try again.

Practice Questions

1) These are the ages of everyone in my family:
68 years, 11 years, 28 years, 9 years, 37 years

What is the median age?

2) These are the scores out of 20 for my maths group's mental arithmetic test:
15, 17, 20, 18, 10

What is the median score?

TOP TIP 1

To remember median think **medium**
Small   **Medium**   Large
(Median is in the middle!)

TOP TIP 2

When there are two numbers in the middle:
-4, 10, 12, 15, 16, 23, 28, 30
find the number that is halfway between them, ie: $15\frac{1}{2}$.

Finding the mode

To achieve Level 5, you need to be able to answer questions on mode.

Just remember: mode is another name for most common value.

Let's try a simple question.

Question: These are the results of sweets in a tube:

46, 47, 46, 49, 42, 45, 45, 46

What is the mode? ☐

1 (Read the question then read it again.)

2 (Think about the question.)

The mode is another name for the most common value.

3 (Picture the numbers.)

Make sets of the same number.

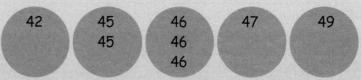

| 42 | 45 45 | 46 46 46 | 47 | 49 |

4 (Double-check.)

Make sure you haven't missed any numbers.

5 (Decide on your answer.)

46 occurs most often.
46 is the mode.

6 (If your answer looks sensible, write it in the box.)

If not, go back to Step 3 and try again.

Practice Question

The children in Year 7 gave marks out of 10 for a particular television programme. These were the marks given:

7.1, 6.9, 3.2, 7.1, 4.6, 4.2, 4.6, 7.1,

7.1, 7.2, 4.9, 5.2, 5.2, 8.4, 7.2, 6.9,

7.1, 6.8, 7.1, 4.6

What was the mode? Mode = ☐

TOP TIP 1

Remember:
Mode is the **Most Common** Value
Modal means **Mode**

TOP TIP 2

Always write out the numbers again and sort them.

Tick off each number so you know you haven't missed any of them. This is IMPORTANT!

Finding the range

To achieve Level 5 you will need to find the range of a series of data.

Just remember: the range is the difference between the lowest and highest value.

Let's try a simple question.

Question: These are the distances 4 students throw a javelin:

27 m , 15 m , 22 m , 8 m

What is the range of these distances? ⬜

1 (Read the question then read it again.)

2 (Think about the question.)   The range is the difference between the lowest and highest value.

3 (Picture the numbers.)   Put them in order: 8, 15, 22, 27.

4 (Study the numbers.)   The furthest distance is 27 m.
The shortest distance is 8 m.
What is the difference between these distances?

5 (Calculate your answer.)   27 m - 8 m = 19 m

6 (If your answer looks sensible, write it in the box.)   If not, go back to Step 3 and try again.

Practice Question

Alton Towers has many visitors. What was the range of visitors for the 1st half of last year?

March	19421	April	32701	May	79206
June	23000	July	35225	August	61527

⬜

TOP TIP 1

When calculating the range ALWAYS write down the numbers again, in order of size.

Graphs and pie charts

To get a Level 5 you will need to look at graphs like the one below and answer questions about them.

Let's try a simple question.

Question: These road signs are in miles. Use the conversion graph to rewrite the road signs in kilometres.

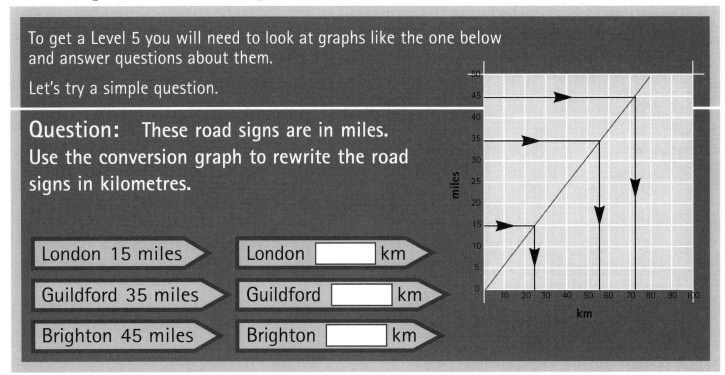

London 15 miles → London ☐ km

Guildford 35 miles → Guildford ☐ km

Brighton 45 miles → Brighton ☐ km

1 (Read the question then read it again.)

Conversion graph tells us that we need to convert values.

2 (Be methodical.)

London
- We need to change 15 miles into kilometres.
- Go up the y axis (miles) and find 15 (halfway between 10 and 20).
- Mark this point on the y axis with your pencil.
- Go across to the conversion line and make another mark.
- Now go down to find out the value in kilometres.
Our answer is 24!
Now repeat for Guildford and Brighton.

3 (Does the answer look sensible? If so, fill in the answer box.)

Check your answers carefully on the graph before writing them in the boxes. The test marker is looking for an EXACT answer.

Practice Questions

1 inch = 2.5cm. Using the graph above to help you, draw a new graph to convert inches to centimetres. Use the graph to find out how much you would receive when you exchange:

1) 7 inches = ☐ cm

2) 12.5 cm = ☐ inches

3) 8.5 inches = ☐ cm

4) 5.5 cm = ☐ inches

Pie charts are circles split up into sections.
To get a Level 5 you need to be able to interpret them.

Question! The pie chart shows the favourite subjects of 18 students.

a) Which was the favourite subject? How can you tell?

b) How many students like Maths?

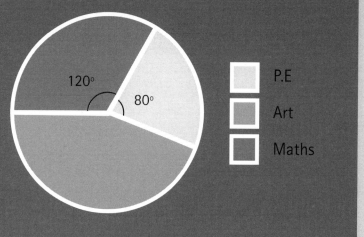

☐ P.E
☐ Art
☐ Maths

1 (Read the question then read it again.)   A pie chart has 360° about the centre.

2 (Answer the questions.)   a) Art was the favourite subject since it has the biggest section.

b) 120° represents the number of students who like Maths.

We write this as a fraction. $120° \div 360° = \frac{1}{3}$

$\frac{1}{3}$ of 18 students like Maths.

$18 \div 3 = 6$ students.

3 (Check that it sounds sensible. If so, write the answers in the box.)   Sounds about right.

Practice Questions

Using the pie chart above, work out how many students like:

1) Art   ☐

2) P.E   ☐

3) How can you check that you have included all the students?

The probability scale

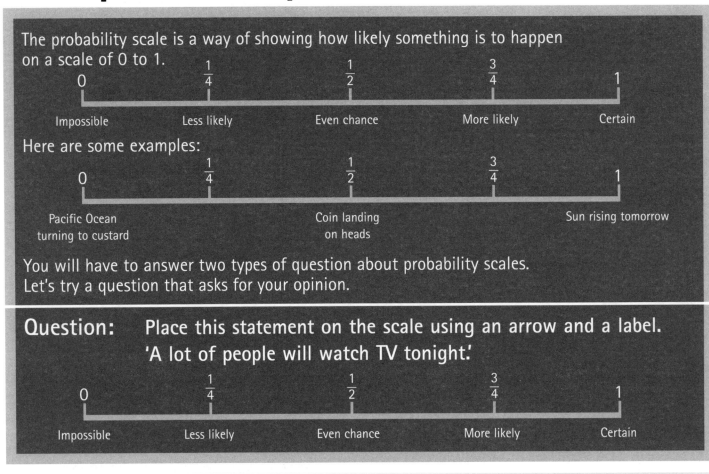

The probability scale is a way of showing how likely something is to happen on a scale of 0 to 1.

Impossible — Less likely — Even chance — More likely — Certain

Here are some examples:

Pacific Ocean turning to custard — Coin landing on heads — Sun rising tomorrow

You will have to answer two types of question about probability scales. Let's try a question that asks for your opinion.

Question: Place this statement on the scale using an arrow and a label. 'A lot of people will watch TV tonight.'

Impossible — Less likely — Even chance — More likely — Certain

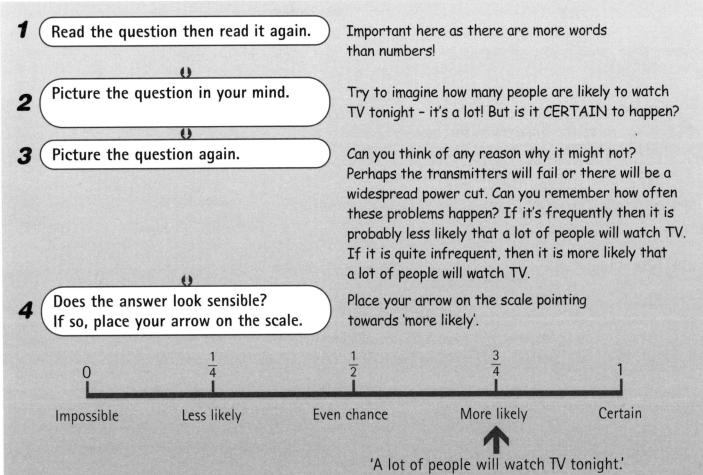

1 Read the question then read it again.

Important here as there are more words than numbers!

2 Picture the question in your mind.

Try to imagine how many people are likely to watch TV tonight – it's a lot! But is it CERTAIN to happen?

3 Picture the question again.

Can you think of any reason why it might not? Perhaps the transmitters will fail or there will be a widespread power cut. Can you remember how often these problems happen? If it's frequently then it is probably less likely that a lot of people will watch TV. If it is quite infrequent, then it is more likely that a lot of people will watch TV.

4 Does the answer look sensible? If so, place your arrow on the scale.

Place your arrow on the scale pointing towards 'more likely'.

Impossible — Less likely — Even chance — More likely — Certain

'A lot of people will watch TV tonight.'

Now let's try a probability question that asks for a mathematically correct answer.

Question! These metal discs are placed in a bag

3 silver, 6 copper, 1 zinc, 2 bronze

Estimate the chance that the first disc to be taken out of the bag is copper and mark it on the probability scale.

1 Read the question then read it again.

Words and numbers to think about.
What is the question asking you to do?

2 Picture the question in your mind.

Try to picture the different discs in the bag.

3 Add up the total number of discs.

3 + 6 + 1 + 2 = 12

4 How many of them are copper?

There are 6 copper discs, so there are 6 copper discs out of 12.

5 Express your probability as a fraction, decimal or percentage. This is important!

This can be expressed as a fraction, percentage or decimal.

$\frac{1}{2}$ 50%   0.5

6 Decide where to place your arrow.

Draw the arrow half way.

7 If your answer checks out, write it in the box.

0	$\frac{1}{4}$	$\frac{1}{2}$	$\frac{3}{4}$	1
Impossible	Less likely	Even chance	More likely	Certain

↑ 'The first disc out of the bag is copper.'

Practice Question

There are 20 pens in a box. 5 don't work, 3 leave blots and the rest work well. What is the probability of picking a pen that works properly?

1) Write your answer as a fraction, decimal or percentage.
2) Draw an arrow on this probability scale as an estimate.

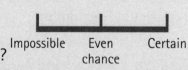

Impossible	Even chance	Certain

'This is the probability that a pen will work.'

TOP TIP 1

When throwing a dice there is an EQUAL chance of rolling any of the numbers. When tossing a coin there is an EQUAL chance of getting heads or tails.

TOP TIP 2

If you are not marking a probability on a scale you must present it as a **fraction**, **decimal** or **percentage**.

Key Facts

Number, Calculations and Algebra

Multiplying decimals by 10, 100 and 1000
- Move numbers to the left.
- Move numbers to the left once when × 10, twice when × 100 and three times when × 1000.

Dividing decimals by 10, 100 and 1000
- Move numbers to the right.
- Move numbers to the right once when ÷ by 10, twice when ÷ by 100, and three times when ÷ by 1000.

Negative numbers
- Integers are just whole numbers.
- When counting from negative up to positive or positive down to negative, **remember to count 0!**
- When counting on a number line, count to the right when adding, count to the left when subtracting.

Decimals to two places
- When rounding, remember 5 is up! $6.785 = 6.79$

Reducing a fraction to its simplest form
- If you are asked to find a proportion or ratio of two things or numbers you are being asked to find a fraction (in its lowest form).

Calculating a fraction or percentage
- Remember as many percentage/fraction equivalents as you can:

$50\% = \frac{1}{2}$ $25\% = \frac{1}{4}$ $75\% = \frac{3}{4}$

$33\% = $ nearly $\frac{1}{3}$ $66\% = $ nearly $\frac{2}{3}$

Multiplication and division (with decimal points)
- × and ÷ are opposites.
- Always estimate first. It will help you to get the decimal point in the right place if one is needed.

Checking your answers
- Inverse means opposite!
- Check addition by subtraction – and vice versa.
- Check division by multiplication – and vice versa.
- Use 'easy numbers' when estimating: 2, 5, 10 etc.

Simple formulae
- **Talk** through the formula in your head. It will make it easier.

Brackets
- Always do brackets in equations first.

Coordinates
- Always read ALONG (x axis) and then UP (y axis).
- Always write (x) before (y) – (x, y).
- Quadrants work **anti-clockwise**.

2nd	1st
3rd	4th

Shape, Space and Measures

2-D shapes

- Pentagon
  Pentagons have FIVE sides.
  Regular pentagons have FIVE EQUAL SIDES.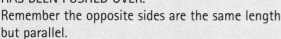

- Parallelogram
  A parallelogram is a RECTANGLE THAT
  HAS BEEN PUSHED OVER.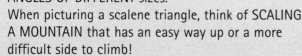
  Remember the opposite sides are the same length
  but parallel.

- Isosceles and scalene triangles
  An isosceles triangle has TWO EQUAL SIDES
  AND TWO EQUAL ANGLES.
  Picture an isosceles triangle as an arrow!
  A scalene triangle has THREE SIDES
  OF DIFFERENT LENGTHS and THREE
  ANGLES OF DIFFERENT sizes.
  When picturing a scalene triangle, think of SCALING
  A MOUNTAIN that has an easy way up or a more
  difficult side to climb!

Angles

- Acute angle lies between 0° and 90°
- Right angle = 90°
- Obtuse angle lies between 90° and 180°
- Straight line = 180°
- Angles around a POINT always
  add up to 360° (a complete turn).
- The angles of a TRIANGLE always
  add up to 180°.

Symmetries

- When drawing reflections, remember to keep
  the correct distance from the mirror line.

Metric and imperial conversions
(approximate)

- 1 litre = 1.8 pints
- 1 kilogram = 2.2 lbs (pounds)
- 1 pound = 0.454 kg
- 1 mile = 1.6 km
- 5 miles = 8 km
- 1 foot = 30 cm
- 1 metre = 3 feet 3 inches
- 1 inch = 2.5 cm

Estimating measures

- Milli = very small
- Centi = small
- Kilo = big

Area of a rectangle

- Area of a rectangle = length (L) × width (W)
- Area is always units squared
  (cm^2, m^2, mm^2)

Handling Data

Pictograms

- With pictograms PICTURE = NUMBER
  e.g.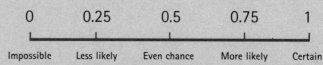

Mean, median, mode, range

- Mean = sum of all numbers divided by
  number of numbers
- Median = middle number in sequence
  (always write down in order first)
- Mode = most common value
- Range = difference between highest
  and lowest number

Charts and graphs

- Be careful and accurate. Use a sharp pencil.
- Pie charts are circles split up into sections.
  Each section represents a certain number
  of articles.

Probability scale

- Always goes from 0 to 1
  (you need fractions/decimals here).

0	0.25	0.5	0.75	1
Impossible	Less likely	Even chance	More likely	Certain

- P (event) = $\dfrac{\text{number of times event occurs}}{\text{total number of outcomes}}$

Tips and technique

Before a test

1 When you revise, try revising 'a little and often' rather than in long sessions.

2 Learn important formulas

3 Learn your multiplication facts up to 10 x 10 so that you can recall them instantly. These are your tools for performing your calculations.

4 Revise with a friend. You can encourage and learn from each other.

5 Get a good night's sleep the night before.

6 Be prepared – bring your own pens and pencils and wear a watch to check the time as you go.

During test

1 Don't rush the first few questions. These tend to be quite straightforward, so don't make any silly mistakes.

2 As you know by now, READ THE QUESTION THEN READ IT AGAIN.

3 If you get stuck, don't linger on the same question – move on! You can come back to it later.

4 Check to see how many marks a question is worth. Have you 'earned' those marks with your answer?

5 Check your answers. You can use the inverse method or the rounding method. Does your answer look correct?

6 Be aware of the time. After 20 minutes, check to see how far you have got.

7 Try to leave a couple of minutes at the end to read through what you have written.

8 Always show your method. You may get a mark for showing you have gone through the correct procedure even if your answer is wrong.

9 Don't leave any questions unanswered. In the two minutes you have left yourself at the end, make an educated guess at the questions you really couldn't do.

The National Tests

Key facts

★ The Key Stage 3 National Tests (or SATs) take place in the middle of May in Year 9. You will be tested on Maths, English and Science.

★ The tests take place in your school and will be marked by examiners – not your teacher!

★ You will get your results in July, two months after you take the tests.

★ Individual test scores are not made public but a school's combined scores are published in what are commonly known as league tables.

The Maths National Tests

You will take three tests in Maths:

Mental Maths Test – This test will be played to you on a CD.
You will have to answer the questions mentally within 5, 10 or 15 seconds.
This test will take about 20 minutes.

Test A – The non-calculator test. This test requires quick answers on a test paper.
You will not be able to use a calculator but should show any working you do.
The test will be one hour long.

Test B – This test allows you to use a calculator and includes problems that will take you longer to solve. The test will be one hour long.

Don't forget!

Using and Applying Mathematics – There will be more questions testing how you use and apply your mathematical knowledge in different situations. This includes: knowing which is the important information in the questions; how to check your results; describing things mathematically using common symbols and diagrams; and explaining your reasons for conclusions that you make.

You might be asked to explain your answers and also write possible answers. Remember to always show your method.

Answers

Level 4 Tricky Bits

Page 8 – Predicting sequences
1) 52, 62   2) 128, 2048   3) 12.5, 6.25

Page 9 – Calculators
1) 1197   2) 107.1   3) 31   4) 529.3   5) 2711.5   6) 3037.5

Page 11 – The 24 hour clock
1) 6hrs and 20 mins   2) 12hrs and 6 minutes   3) 6hrs and 44 minutes   4) 1hr and 21 minutes

Page 12 – Reading scales
1) 70 ml   2) 190 ml

Page 13 – Multiples, factors and primes
a) 12, 18, 24, 36   b) 7, 13, 37   c) 1, 15

Level 5

Page 14 – Checking your answers
1) 3654   2) 1789   3) 84   4) 8465

Page 15 – Checking your answers
1) 6256   2) 4315   3) 188   4) 41.8

Page 17 – Multiplying and dividing by 10, 100 and 1000
1) 420   2) 100   3) 9   4) 0.31
5) 10   6) 7.2

Page 19 – Decimals
1) 23.59   2) £11.92   3) 27.35   4) £25.50

Page 20 – Reducing fractions
1) $\frac{3}{4}$ 2) $\frac{1}{3}$ 3) $\frac{6}{7}$ 4) $\frac{7}{8}$

Page 21 – Ratio and proportion
1) 2:3   2) $\frac{3}{5}$

Page 23 – Calculating fractions or percentages
Practice questions 1
1) £100   2) 27 cm   3) 27 g   4) 770 ml   5) 93.5 km   6)84 cm

Practice questions 2
1) £25   2) 63 g   3) 55 ml   4) 56 m

Page 25 – Multiplication and division
1) 13   2) 13   3) 16   4) 11382   5) 65072   6) 36

Page 27 – Negative numbers

1) –6°, –2°, 0°, 3°, 4°   2) –46, –33, –31, 18, 27

3) 5 hours   4) 20°

Page 29 – Simple formulae

1) T = £96   2) N = 4   3) P = £16

Formula L = (W × 5) + 12 = 5W + 12

Page 31 – Number and Algebra

1a) 7a – b   b) 4b – 4a   c) 5m + n

Name	Age
John	y
Kate	y + 2
Alfie	y – 5
Sara	2y

Page 34 – Coordinates

1) (–4, –3) = 3rd Quadrant   (–5, 3) = 2nd Quadrant   (3, 2) = 1st Quadrant

2) (1, 0) (2, –2) (5, –2) (4, 0)

Page 35 – Angles

(a) 80°   (b) 142°   (c) 215°

Page 36 – Angles

(a) 47°   (b) 73°   (c) 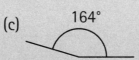 164°

Page 37 – Angles

(a) 45°   (b) 45°   (c) 25°

Page 39 – Angles

1) (a) 15°   (b) 50°   (c) 72°

2) (a) 288°   (b) 250°   (c) 332°

3) (a) 90° – right angle   (b) 135° (approx) – obtuse angle

   (c) 225° (approx) – reflex angle   (d) 45° (approx) – acute angle

4) 85°   5) 55°

Page 42 – Symmetries of 2D shapes

1) (a) 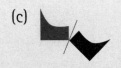 (b) 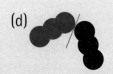 (c) (d) (e) (f)

2) (a) ✗   (b) ✓ order 4   (c) ✗   (d) ✓ order 6

Page 43 – Symmetries of 2D shapes

3) (a) ✓ 1 to right, 4 down   (b) ✓ 3 to right, 3 down   (c) ✗

(d) ✓ 5 to right, 2 down   (e) ✓ 1 to right, 3 up   (f) ✗

Page 44 – Metric equivalents of imperial units

1) $17\frac{1}{2}$ pints   2) 56 kilometres

Page 45 – Metric equivalents of imperial units

1) 1500 ml   2) 3.97 tonnes   3) 375 lengths

Page 47 – Estimating with measures

1) (a) – (d) These will vary in estimates and actual measures dependent on your book, table, classroom and sports hall!

2) (a) kilograms   (b) kilometres   (c) litres   (d) grams   (e) millimetres
   (f) centilitres   (g) tonnes   (h) metres   (i) millilitres

Page 49 – Finding the area of a rectangle

1) 1400 m²   2) 142 km²

Page 50 – Finding the mean

1) 5.3   2) 91.5   3) 23.17   4) 3.5

Page 51 – Finding the median

1) 28 years   2) 17

Page 52 – Finding the mode

Modal mark = 7.1

Page 53 – Finding the range

Range of visitors = 59 785 visitors

Page 54 – Interpreting graphs and pie charts

1) 17.5 cm   2) 5 inches   3) 21.25 cm   4) 2.2 inches

Page 55 – Interpreting graphs and pie charts

1) 8 students   2) 4 students

3) Since there are 18 students in total, Art – 8, PE – 4 and Maths – 6.
All students have been included.

Page 57 – Probabilities

1) $\frac{3}{5}$ or 60% or 0.6   2)

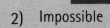

Impossible   Even   Certain
chance